A Scythe of Moon

A Scythe of Moon

Poems by

June Blumenson

© 2020 June Blumenson. All rights reserved.
This material may not be reproduced in any form, published,
reprinted, recorded, performed, broadcast,
rewritten or redistributed without
the explicit permission of June Blumenson.
All such actions are strictly prohibited by law.

Cover design by Shay Culligan

Photograph by Justin Campbell

ISBN: 978-1-950462-61-2

Kelsay Books Inc.

kelsaybooks.com

502 S 1040 E, A119
American Fork, Utah 84003

For Paula

Acknowledgments

The author thanks the publications in which the following poems, sometimes in earlier versions, first appeared.

Adanna Literary Journal: Women and War. (2013)
    Let Me Count
    Fugu
Boston Literary Magazine. (2009)
    Riding a Hog
Comstock Review. (2015)
    Cabbages and Kings
Earth's Daughters. (Fall 2016)
    Water Tones
Gyroscope Review. (Fall 2018)
    Eulogy for Fishnets
    Vortex of Sedona
Literal Latte. (2015)
    Relics
San Pedro River Review. Blue Horse Press. (Spring 2016)
    The Night We Ate the Javelina
The Edge: (2011)
    Barely October
The French Literary Review: Issue No.18. (2012)
    Mot Juste
The Poet's Billow: (2016)
    Lament (Previously entitled Ode to a Glacier.)
When Time and Space Conspire. (2017)
    A Scythe of Moon
    A Dog's Life
    Ancestral Dreams
    Stuff of Wounds

Contents

I

A Scythe of Moon	13
The Night We Ate the Javelina	14
I Disassemble	16
Relics	17
What's in Her Journal	20
Sisters' Reunion	21
Mot Juste	22
Black Fabric of Space	23
Ancestral Dream	24

II

Stuff of Wounds	27
Let Me Count	28
It's Barely October	29
Fugu	30
Lament	31
All Aboard	32
Making Tracks	33
Muses of the Lower World	34
Vortex of Sedona	35

III

Burgeoning	39
Atlas Shrugged	40
Riding a Hog	41
Beauty and the Beast	42
The Scent of a Man	43
A Dog's Life	44
Password	45
Spring Equinox	46

IV

Cabbages and Kings	49
Water Tones	50
Magician's Sleeve	51
Annual Exam	52
Color of the Year	53
Eulogy for Fishnets	54
Winter's Womb	55

I

A Scythe of Moon

You don't have to be a house
to be haunted or breathe
stagnant air of abandoned places
where beasts go bump in the night
and you wake to eat the cold.
You have only to witness
a thump in your chest, old haunts
scented with rosemary, lemon
poppy-seed cake you still taste,
wind ruffling your hair.

You don't have to climb attic
stairs in search of specters
settled in dust. You have only
to receive the sun's burst
upon your shoulder
or your dead mother's arms
that embrace you when you sit
in her chair. People we love
run under our skin. They stretch
and grin inside us, crack us open,
reveal a scythe of moon.

The Night We Ate the Javelina

I watched you take small bites
and tip your chin down
to make it easier to swallow.
What do you think about?
I asked. Tea-lights flickered
in your cactus garden, plants
christened by a happy
heart, a full belly, selected
for heat tolerance—golden
barrels, Mexican fence posts,
and clumps of prickly pear
from which (we always said)
we will someday
make honey. You said,
I think about my limitations.

I thought about the javelina,
its spear-like teeth
that sharpen when the mouth opens
and closes, how mothers roll
and tumble their young,
their short life span, salt
and pepper hair, spiky ruffs
around their necks;
how you don't have to bleed
the javelina when dressing the carcass;
how your friend expertly butchered
and kept the roast he gave us clean.

I thought about how you might choke
on wild meat and let it marinate
while I pushed you in your wheelchair
in the desert botanical garden.
I thought about how the javelina leaves
its scent on rocks and tree stumps,
and how we'd probably never
make honey out of prickly pear.

I Disassemble

the small cairn we'd placed
on the altar, worrying
the stones between my fingers.
Coffee cups are drained,
the table's bounty reduced
to scraps. The last few mourners

straggle out the door
leaving behind a wake
of affection. Seamless how
the intimate gathering came

together. It has been a long day.
Dishes washed, extra chairs
folded away. The sun
not yet set. It is possible
to have too much daylight.

I welcome shorter days
when time falls backward,
long nights when
I will reassemble. I always
imagine I will be wiser in winter.

Relics

i

After
she was in the ground,
sent off to,
god knows where,
we returned to the house
and sorted through
the scent
of her.

ii

Our inheritance,
like medicine,
had been dispensed
long before.

iii

I got the china,
her original
wedding band.
Too big
for my finger,
it slid free
down
the drain.

iv

Later my sister said,
She told me
you
were
her favorite.

v

I sank
into the edge
of my parents' bed,
not even pulling
back the hand crocheted
bedspread,
as we were taught,
could barely mumble,
I never
once
felt
that.

vi

It was as if
my mother and I,
like forgotten pots
boiling
on the back burner,
had reduced each other
to vapor.

vii

Could it have been
we stood
our whole lives,
a solid-core door
between us,
each of us
on opposite sides
screaming,
let
me
in?

viii

After
the funeral,
I took my sister's words,
like bits
of bone, clipped nails,
a strand
of hair,
and packed up
my car trunk
with them,
not knowing what
to do
with them.

What's in Her Journal

Vintage beads. A brilliance
for secrecy. Private details
of love. Distorted fragments
of dreams spilled
on her pillow—great aunt
Kathryn's disparate eyes
(one brown, the other blue),
Grandma's elongated
earlobes, her mother's polio-
twisted leg. A lost child.
Flawed characters.
Her brothers' toy-soldiers.
Paper-dolls shopping
for hand-drawn clothes.
Coded confessions.
Gladiolas in a tall vase.
An inner sanctum of grief.
Forgiveness. Grace.

Sisters' Reunion

I sit at the island counter, a red splash
of tomatoes at my elbow, watch
my older sisters buzz with legendary
efficiency. One peels hard-boiled eggs,
the other rolls crusts for rhubarb pies.

We talk of our parents' old house
hoisted on a flatbed and moved,
furnishings inside intact—pictures,
drapes, even dishes and colored
glass bottles of cheap perfume.

I slept upstairs on a cot in an open
dormer, a hallway really, between
my sisters' room and the room
my three older brothers shared. I'd hear
muffled laughter, words mumbled
through walls in the night as I sang
to myself by light of the moon.

In the morning, I'd wake to a parade
of them clomping through my corridor,
racing to see who could jump
down the most stairs without falling.

My sisters bustle amidst biscuits.
One chops onions and potatoes,
the other whisks cream. They widen
their circle. *You can slice up the tomatoes,*
the oldest says, and I step in.

Mot Juste

Pour Genevieve, ma belle- mère française

We kissed the air
when we'd meet,
cheek to cheek,
soft as the inside
of a lamb's ear,
the wrist's faint pulse,
a handful of water,
a hint of herbs
and *Chanel* brushing
between us,
the sound of love
in her throat,
like an ocean's
white wave.

She was midnight,
a waltz, the black
dress, exquisite
as French lace,
cut glass catching
in candlelight,
fraise des bois
in a flute of champagne.
She was an ornate
invitation,
an evening well spent.

Black Fabric of Space

As a child I welcomed cold, northern
lights, stabs of frigid inhalation, fumes
of curled breath, and icicles brandished

like daggers in the sun. How playful,
my little life, compared to grandmothers
during Russian winters—the quality

of light sobering as they braced
against wind-swept steppes dreaming
of a new world. Steel skies, cataract

visions, how it must have been the day
before creation when stars collapsed
into holes ripped in the black fabric
of space, then shattered into showers of light.

Ancestral Dream

She'd come undone, sprang out of a wall cloud, her hair dripping tornados. And she squeezed and squeezed curls until she'd wrung-out all the weather. It overflowed onto the floor—the long voice of a violin sobbing elsewhere. Don't, I shouted to this phantom when she brandished a knife and started to dig dirt from under the tile, prying it up in bits and pieces. I heard dry catgut strings snap—metal wound so tight on that old fake Stradivarius. My grandfather sat upin his coffin, stared into the white night, music in his belly weeping, still afraid the Czar's army, even in death, would catch him running away to Brazil.

II

Stuff of Wounds

If I were an alchemist,
I would conjure
rubies from the flame,
change dust into magic
powders, teach time to stay,
transform the world
into a place where trees
never lose their leaves,
and dreams
do not have wings.

The stuff of wounds
would turn to silk,
every broken promise
would find repair,
and all the bitter
in the mouth
would melt into elixir,
sweet and full
as golden peaches,
and all the bones
we pick from ashes,
would be made whole.

Let Me Count

When my oldest brother was killed
by fifty years of smoking,
long after he survived the Korean
Conflict, the Forgotten War,
(sandwiched as it is in between
other greater wars,
as if some wars are more worthy
of memory than others)
I stood at the foot of his grave,
jolted by a three-gun salute.

Which war is mine to claim,
I wondered—the one I was born
into or Vietnam, my rite
of passage or the war on terror
I never imagined I'd see.
My mother died during the Kosovo
War, known as the good war,
peacefully in her home.
She outlived her first born.

How do I love you? Let me count
the wars we've lived through.
I still have exotic stamps
from letters and silk pajamas,
embroidered with fuchsia flowers,
my brother sent
from Korea when I was four.

It's Barely October

and ash leaves fall straight down
like parachutes above a battlefield,
landing on a dusting of snow
that coats the deck white,
drapes an open umbrella, blankets
pots of blooming begonia.

We think we know when things
are supposed to happen,
bemoan unseasonable frost,
presume spring is late,
proclaim the baby came too early.

Green leaves line patio lounge-chairs
like bodies of young soldiers
caught without winter boots,
dressed in khaki not even thinking
of winter—like sandals still strewn
on the entryway floor, closets
still full of summer jackets.

Fugu

deadly Pacific balloon fish

No Alaskan cruise ship for me, even if wilderness
guides don't carry guns, or so I thought until
our guide, in hip boots, swung her legs
over the side of the raft and pushed us off
under noses of bears jumping for salmon in the Kenai.

And when we landed in the backcountry
and began an ascent up the mountain, she called out
her warning, *Hey, bear,* then stepped over fresh
tracks the size of baseball gloves, scat huge and blue.

Surrounded by a multitude of lichen that lined rocky
slopes like galleries of primordial paintings, we clomped
through hemlock forests, catching a glimpse of the peak
where patches of snow hung around all summer.

It was then I remembered white balloons. World War II
surprise packages like piñatas floating over the sea
from Japan, landing in trees and tundra, carrying
payloads of explosives. *Weather balloons,* the army said,

so as not to panic people, thousands of balloon bombs
like a school of fugu flying over the ocean—only
three hundred recovered, others still out there
in forests, deserts, lakes and mountains.
Unexploded ordnance from Alaska to Mexico.

Lament

It isn't the vast, ridged
ice field, pyramidal peaks,
nor how a glacier
inches forward, en masse
like a river of ice,
that overwhelms me.
It's the angry sound
of exploding chunks
of ice-face that calve
into the sea,
the thunderous roar
against human footprints
spewing putrid
breath into our air
like pods of spouting whales.

We fly to vanishing
places, ignore the impact
of a seat on a plane,
plant trees as carbon
credit for our stateroom
with a view, snap
pictures of a last
glance of a lifetime—
tufted puffins
dive-bomb for fish,
water glistens
off splashing seals.
An arctic fox
on an iceberg drifts out to sea.

All Aboard

On a hot, humid day on a train bound
for Chicago, lulled senseless by rhythms
of steel against steel, the hoarse whistle
announcing crossroads. I met America.

We stared at each other through the train's
dirty windows. I witnessed the homeless
beneath trestles, gang graffiti, waste
of the heartland, rusted out machinery
and stacks of goin' nowhere blown out tires.

I saw a worried landscape along the spine
of the railbed, not what those who long
for a new world come here to see.
I turned to look out the other window,
away from the raw side toward pastures,
ballparks, sky-scraping towers, power grids,
corporate castles, mosques, synagogues

and steeples. Then I turned to immigrant
faces in rows around me, all bound
for somewhere, traveling the divide—
heard rails squealing, steam
hissing as we rolled into the station,
the baritone whistle announcing America.

Making Tracks

i

On a quiet suburban street
where only chimney smoke mingles,
a young woman emerges
from her doorstep, brushes snowflakes
from her headscarf, her face
bejeweled by morning sun.
Nobody takes a bus to work
in this neighborhood but there she goes.

ii

At night when the neighborhood
can't sleep, it googles hijab,
burqa, Sharia law,
Middle Eastern recipes and spices.

iii

From the other end of the block,
a tall stately woman, dressed
in a blue abaya, pushes
her bundled-up baby in a stroller,
string bag dangles from her shoulder.
Nobody walks to a grocery store
in this neighborhood, but there she goes.
Thin-wheeled tracks zigzag in hard-crusted snow.

Muses of the Lower World

They come in leaky boats,
lured by songs of sirens,
leap into temptress waters
trying to reach the shore.

*Womens, childrens
and they don't know swim,*
a Greek fisherman says,
counting washed up bodies,

collecting splintered ribs
of boats on the shore.
Homelands recede behind
them, futures compromised

or vanished, still they come
to the swallowing sea,
heed boasts of sirens,
trills of promise and dare.

Vortex of Sedona

I lick salt from the rim of margaritas
as if it were   earth
nibble crackers   sautéed sweet
potatoes   watch an older woman spin
heavy trays of cocktails

what are her bowls of bad
luck   choice of olives
sun-dried tomatoes   I study
the fashionistas   envy stilettos

Suddenly I am exhausted
invisible
a vortex swirling   down the drain

I take one long last sip
I am not like ancient people
whom it is said
could live without water in the desert

I leave the waitress a huge tip
conspire to jump
into the hotel fountain   turbulent as prayer

III

Burgeoning

At seventeen, I was blue-sky, don't look back, fly-me-to-the-moon weightless but for pockets full of *On the Road* and poems of passion. I was *The Fountainhead*. I shrugged—my trunk packed with a statue of Buddha and a bust with a Roman nose I called Marcus Aurelius. The stoic emperor said, *...live each day as if it were your last without pretense, stupor, or agitation.* But I was all about pretending, the world in a cold stupor. And no more big brother flinging his coat over my head at scary movies, my arms an agitating pinwheel to be free. I ate breakfast at Tiffany's. Bricks were laid to build the Berlin Wall. The first Freedom Riders challenged Jim Crow. A Soviet cosmonaut flew into space, and *Don't let it be forgot, that for one brief, shining moment there was Camelot.* When I was seventeen.

Atlas Shrugged

Anxious to get the last one grown,
her parents ignored late night
hours, shrugged off her wanton look,
footprints in the snow outside
her bedroom window. And love,

wedged like a foot in the door
of knowledge, ran naked caught up
in bad poetry and coney islands
of the mind. The simple eloquence
of you is quite enough, her boyfriend
said. To be in love was everything,

mystic language of eyes and hands,
torn sentences of passion
that defied convention throwing off
the weight of the world.
Love was easy, unburdened, like that.

Riding a Hog

I don't know what got into me that day
when I decided to hop on the back
of a Harley without a helmet
and go for a cold beer. I suppose
I could blame it on the fact
that I wasn't carrying
too much stuff to refuse
the offer, had no real excuse, still,
I could have said no—

to this man, the next door neighbor,
who I knew could not hold his cards
worth a damn, always folded,
had the worst luck
ever, and, besides that, he was well
into his eighties, Santa Claus cheeks,
but still strong with a twinkle in his eyes
as if he knew something I didn't.

Before I got to know him, I saw him taking off
for weekend rides in black leathers,
leaving his wife behind, who shook her head.
They'd made their deal.
Saw him as a kind of Jekyll, a sort of Mr. Hyde.

Later when I told a friend about him,
she asked, *Did that really happen?* I smiled
seeing the predicament
in her eyes, trying to work it out, caught
somewhere between belief and doubt.
When I didn't answer, she narrowed her eyes
and said, *You're such a—Mona Lisa.*

Beauty and the Beast

So what if the cow
doesn't jump over the moon,
the glass slipper never finds
its match, the duckling
rarely becomes a swan.

We give it a shot
to the head outside of reason
nibbling on the candied
roof of the hut tucked deep
in the forest.

*Bread crumbs add up and rags
turn to riches,* says the fairy
godmother, staring down
the long nose of romance.

So what if the magic wand
is rusty, the apple nearly kills us,
and love is a feather. We skip
upon fields picking bouquets
of wild dill. The earth blue.

The Scent of a Man

should be like fresh-sawn oak,
aged and warmed by sunbeams,
just a hint of smoke and vanilla
dabbed behind each ear.

It should keep you summery
for a lifetime. Palm fronds,
a film of sea salt on skin,
hot metal aroma of outer space—

scents that transport you
to the Italian villa of your mind
where you throw open
the shutters and shout down

to the courtyard, *amore.* Saffron,
coastal blossoms, cracked pepper
and coriander leaves soaked
in fennel brine. Crystalized thyme.

A Dog's Life

Instantly, he jumped up to nestle
his head against her neck,
(forgetting his noble lineage)
rolled over and sat on her feet—
happy he was to see his mistress
from a past lifetime
in another perfect human rebirth.

At first she did not know him
but when they looked
into each other's eyes, greetings
of ten thousand souls
reverberated between them.
So tender was her scratch
behind his ears, so softly she said,
Ah, my loyal friend. He heard
longing in her voice,
the rasp of time, the wear
of too many dog years of despair.

What had happened to them over years?
All he knew was that not one lifetime
went by that he did not think of her,
wonder what sign she would give him,
how he would know her,
so he could show her his love again.

Password

If I tell ya, I'll have to kill ya,
a coworker said every time I skipped
a staff meeting and asked him
for the news. Claimed he did special
CIA missions, always wore dark glasses.

He slipped me a formula to select
passwords. *Sorry, if I tell ya,
I'll have to kill ya,* because I use
the same security question for everything.
Who was your childhood best friend?

Her name was M******.
An army brat. She'd traveled everywhere,
not only knew names of all the state
capitols but had posed for photos
beneath the lofty domes, had soap bars
and miniature bottles of shampoo
from hotels all over the world.
We formed a clandestine club,
Just Us Girls Society—code JUGS.
The boys on the playground laughed.

When I slept at her house, her mother
French braided her hair
and served soft boiled eggs
in Russian doll cups for breakfast.
These were my people.
In third grade, she moved away, left me
with wanderlust. I kept her name.
If I tell ya, I'll have to kill ya.

Spring Equinox

that curious time, when the sun,
as if birthing light, pushes
toward the earth,
and night and day, full-fledged
companions, consummate
a time when neither triumphs,
when that equiponderous moment
almost makes us believe
balance can exist.

I clamor for spring,
applaud when day outgrows
the night, gives light
more weight,
renews the force of dawn.

I know that life and death need
each other; but still, like Eve,
when she could not wrestle
darkness to the ground,
like her when she cried out
to Adam, I cry out to spring,
how glad I am to see your face.

IV

Cabbages and Kings

I wonder what Monet, obsessed
with changing light,
would see if he wandered into my garden
to sit with me en plein air.
Would we sip wine, talk of shadows captured
like caged fireflies gone dim.
Would he illuminate my single view
helpless to each stroke of time,
each brush of dark and dappled light.

Would I ask him where have all the people
gone in his painted streets
and beaches, and when did this place
of cabbages and kings
pull us to the must
of earth, the turn of worms—when
did this solitary place become enough?

Water Tones

Lake Superior

If only I could send you the modulations
of water, the deep pitch of inrush,
the outflow, how waves, like a conversation

keep going, talking over and past
each other, crashing against rocks head-on,
relentless ripples, churned-up foam.

If only I could send you yesterday,
a different timbre
when rain-filled tide pools shimmered

on the sunlit shore and a white gull glided
so gracefully on unbroken water
that I took it for a swan.

Magician's Sleeve

I miss the long days of summer
when every agony
was nourished, inched
toward resolve, lingered
like oak leaves late into the season,
and all the stories
I told seemed worth
repeating, voluminized—my world
so elemental
I hardly perceived gray
undertones—ashes, breath, fog, clay.

I miss when color swept
like scarves from a magician's
sleeve was so primary
I saw only red,
yellow, blue—
midnight embers, Mediterranean
skies, fields of sunflowers,
tinctures of earth, wind, flint, rain.

Annual Exam

I'm testy—every year probed,
poked to see if I'm up to muster.
Bones, bowels, breasts run through
a wringer. Lab work, memory
tests, monitors for blood pressure.
Reoccurring nightmares of college
exams. Did I pass? Did I fail?

I'm asked to draw a clock—hands
on with the big here, the long now.
Haven't they heard the world's gone
digital. I'm beginning to hear
the silence everything takes on.
It's harder to adjust to dark.

There are new memory words
on the exam this year. V*illage,
baby, kitchen.* But I'm comforted
by the past and sticking with
a banana, the sunrise, a chair.

Color of the Year

Forget blue.
Deep, moody,
endless
reflecting pools.
This year
the hue is earthy.
Primrose
in a pot of clay.
Moth wings,
roasted chestnuts,
peach parfait.

Forget blueprints,
cracked
robins' eggs,
last year's blue
moons. Embrace
eraser-pink,
ear-to-the-shell
beaches, the salmon
run, golden
retrievers,
shifting dunes.

Eulogy for Fishnets

I slip my feet into the legs
of pantyhose, slowly
roll the netting over my ankles,
my shins, my thighs,
and slither the black seams
up the back of my legs to end
perfectly straight like cast fishing lines.
Such care, such precision would serve
other parts of my life as well.
The diamond-shaped mesh digs
into my flesh as I step into tap shoes.

What madness to come late to the dance,
net a dream that likens a charmed fish
with sequined scales—my body, an oar
pivoting around its lock—sheer
audacity calibrating
my arms, my legs, my weight.

After the last dance, I cleanse
my stockings like a corpse
prepared for viewing. The black dye
bleeds and darkens the basin.
I hang them outside to dry
kicking in their empty casing.
It is right to acknowledge the dead.
No one can take from me what I have danced.

Winter's Womb

In winter, when heartbeats slow
to a murmur, I imagine the Great Bear
shaking the heavens causing stars to shoot

and fall continents away where I stand
wishing upon constellations—wishing
for a skylark chorus, a crocus to push

through snow. I muster a trust in spring,
in long labor, because that is what spring
does, trusts the motherhood of nature,

the rush of broken waters. And every
year, I stagger into spring like a bear
drunk from deep heart slumber,
through snowmelt to tall, slender grass.

With Special Thanks

to Karen Kelsay of Kelsay Books for catapulting *A Scythe of Moon* into the world. I thank Joyce Sutphen, Minnesota Poet Laureate for her support and poets/editors Sharon Chmielarz and Chet Corey for their close attention to the manuscript. I applaud Loft Literary Center instructors, especially Jude Nutter and Deborah Keenan; Banfill-Locke Center for the Arts writers-in-residence: Kirsten Dierking, Kris Bigalk, Gary Dop, and Silverwood poets: Carol Rusk, Mary Moore Easter, Kathe Warneke and Marlene Jezierski for consistent feedback. I am grateful for friendship and keen eyes of my readers, Carol Bender and Elizabeth Weir, and my lifetime friend, Mary Lynne Bergh. A shout of appreciation for many other cheerleaders who show up and sustain me, especially Kathryn Frommer, Sandra Kacher, Pamm Smith, Michael Diaz, Vicky Dillavou, Karen Wahlund, Kat Bernhoft, Kathy Hawkins, Linda Johnson, Gretchen Pinsonneault and the rest of the Poetry Club gang. Big love to my daughter Paula and sister Audrey for sharing my publication happiness, and my husband, Nick, who usually sits in the back row at readings and says to anyone who will listen, "She's the best."

About the Author

June Blumenson curates a poetry reading series, facilitates poetry writing workshops and is a member of Minnesota Poetry Therapy Network. Her work appears in dozens of literary journals including Comstock, Literal Latte, San Pedro River Review. She was a finalist for Nimrod's Pablo Neruda Prize for Poetry and received the Loft/MIA Sacred Shorts Writing Contest Award.

She left North Dakota (miscast in a northern drama) to bake in the Florida sun at the University of Miami, received degrees in English and psychology from George Washington University and interned as a psycho-dramatist at St. Elizabeth's Hospital in Washington, D.C. After working many years in Toronto as a youth counselor, she returned to the mid-west to settle in Minneapolis where she received an M.A. in Human Resources Development from St. Thomas University and pursued a career providing, developing and administering mental health services.

She has written screen plays, novels and creative nonfiction. *A Scythe of Moon* is her debut collection of poetry. She is often sighted walking around Lake Harriet with her husband Nick or daughter Paula and four-legged Theo.

www.ingramcontent.com/pod-product-compliance
Lightning Source LLC
LaVergne TN
LVHW091320080426
835510LV00007B/573